EAST BAY
THEN & NOW

EAST BAY THEN & NOW

DENNIS EVANOSKY AND ERIC J. KOS

San Diego, California

Thunder Bay Press
An imprint of the Advantage Publishers Group
5880 Oberlin Drive, San Diego, CA 92121-4794
www.thunderbaybooks.com

PRC Publishing
The Chrysalis Building
Bramley Road, London W10 6SP, United Kingdom

An imprint of **Chrysalis** Books Group plc

© 2004 PRC Publishing

ISBN-13: 978-1-59223-350-2
ISBN-10: 1-59223-350-3

Library of Congress Cataloging-in-Publication Data
Evanosky, Dennis.
   East Bay then & now / Dennis Evanosky and Eric J. Kos.
      p. cm.
   ISBN 1-59223-350-3
   1. East Bay (Calif.)--Pictorial works. 2. East Bay (Calif.)--History--Pictorial Works. I.
Title: East Bay then and now II. Kos, Eric J. III. Title.

F868.E22E93 2005
979.4'65'0022-dc22

2004053737

Printed and bound in China

2 3 4 5 09 08 07 06 05

Acknowledgments:

We dedicate this book to David J. McIntyre (1937–2004). Thanks for the view.

We would also like to thank the following people for their help: Fremont: Regina Dennie, Natalie K.
Munn. Hayward: Bernie Columb. Castro Valley: Ken O'Donnell. San Leandro: Cindy Simons. Alameda:
Woody Minor, Nancy Hird, and Robb Ratto. We would like to especially thank Harbormaster Tony Fraga
for allowing us access to the top of the silo on his property. Oakland: Steve Lavoie, Katherine Leles
DiGiovanni, Annalee Allen, and Betty Marvin. Piedmont: Gail Lombardi and Ann Swift. Berkeley: Tom
Edwards. El Cerrito and Albany: The staff of the Contra Costa History Museum in Martinez and Chris
Treadway. Richmond: Donald Bastin. Point Richmond: Gary Shows.

The following sources were used in the writing of this book: *City of Fremont: The First 30 Years* by the City
of Fremont; *Hayward: Heart of the Bay* by Banning Fenton; *San Leandro: A Garden Grows in Eden* by Harry
E. Shaffer; *Alameda: A Geographical History* by Imelda Merlin; *Alameda Heritage Days: 1978 Souvenir Album*
by Mary Rudge; *Historic Commercial Buildings of Alameda* by Woodruff C. Minor; *Pacific Gateway: An
Illustrated History of the Port of Oakland* by Woodruff C. Minor; *Oakland: The Story of a City* by Beth
Bagwell, Oakland Heritage Alliance Newsletters; *Exactly Opposite the Golden Gate* by Phil McArdle;
Berkeley Landmarks by Susan Dinkelspiel Cerny; *Picturing Berkeley: A Postcard History* by Burl Willles;
Berkeley: A City in History by Charles Wollenberg; *Images of America: Richmond* by Donald Bastin; *Regional:
History of Alameda County, California* by Myron Winslow Wood; *A Living Legacy: Historic Architecture of the
East Bay* by Mark A. Wilson; *Alameda County: California Crossroads* by Ruth Hendricks Willard;
Courthouses of California by Ray McDevitt; and *California Railroads* by Alvin A. Fickewirth.

Picture Credits:

The publisher wishes to thank the following for kindly supplying the photographs that appear in this book:

Then photographs:
© Authors' collection 98.
© Alameda Museum 38, 40, 42, 44, 46, 48, 50, 52, 54, 58.
© Berkeley Historical Society 110, 112, 114, 120, 124.
© Contra Costa County Historical Society 128, 130.
© City of Piedmont 60, 60 (inset)
© Corbis / Bettmann 116, 116 (inset) / Ted Streshinsky 118.
© Emeryville Historical Society 62, 64.
© Hayward Area Historical Society 12, 14, 16, 18, 20.
© Lucille Lorge 22.
© Robert B. Fisher Collection / Museum of Local History, Freemont 6, 8, 10.
© Oakland Public Library, Oakland History Room 1, 28, 36, 56, 66, 68, 70, 72, 74, 78, 80, 82, 84, 86, 88,
90, 92, 94, 96, 100, 100 (inset), 102, 104, 106, 106 (inset), 108, 122, 126.
© Richmond Museum of History 132, 134, 136, 138, 140, 142.
© San Leandro Public Library 24, 26, 30, 32, 34.

Now Photographs:
All photographs were taken by Simon Clay (© Chrysalis Image Library), apart from the following:
© Corbis: Mark E. Gibson 117 / Robert Holmes 119.
© Dennis Evanosky 127.

INTRODUCTION

The East Bay describes a geographic, rather than a political, entity. Originally known as Contra Costa (the opposite shore), the region's northernmost portion has a slice of county with that original name. Most of the East Bay lies in Alameda County, named for the creek that meanders through the southern East Bay and empties into San Francisco Bay.

This look at the East Bay begins in the south with the region's youngest city, Fremont, which was founded in 1956 by incorporating five nineteenth-century villages that later grew into towns: Mission San Jose, Niles, Irvington, Centerville, and Warm Springs.

Spaniards first appeared on the scene in 1772, and again in 1776 when they sent their soldiers and priests to settle the region. The Franciscans gave European culture its East Bay birth at Mission San Jose. When the Mexican government declared its independence from Spain in 1820, it began to reward its friends with land grants they called *ranchos*. Just before the Mexican declaration, a retired soldier, Luis Maria Peralta, managed to acquire 144,000 acres in the heart of the East Bay. Others soon followed: Andreas Pico and Juan Alvarado each received 30,000 acres, Jose de Jesus Vallejo 17,000 acres, and Joaquin Estudillo 6,830 acres. In 1834, the Mexican government secularized mission lands, leaving more precious real estate to distribute. They offered some of the land to foreigners. In 1846, a group of Mormons arrived and settled near Mission San Jose. They planted wheat and fruit and prospered.

On the morning of January 24, 1848, just one hundred miles to the north, James Marshall was inspecting a ditch at John Sutter's sawmill on the American River when a sparkle in the water caught his eye. He picked up a glittering particle half the size of a pea. It was a discovery that would change California forever: gold.

At first Marshall's discovery impressed no one. The following year, Samuel Brannan, who had arrived in California with the Mormons, returned from the gold fields and paraded his finds through the streets of San Francisco. "Gold, gold on the American River," he cried. This time, word of the discovery spread like fire.

Gold transformed Contra Costa's bucolic farmlands into a bustling region full of people, many either going to or coming from the gold fields. Some disappointed forty-niners chose to stay; villages became towns and towns became cities. These newcomers laid out new settlements where once there were none. Gideon Aughinbaugh and William Chipman purchased and began developing the Alameda peninsula in 1851. The next year, Horace Carpentier, Andrew Moon, and Edson Adams laid out the town of Oakland. Captain James H. Jacobs put down roots on the bay near Strawberry Creek in 1853—the area would become Ocean View and Albany. In 1853 San Francisco butcher John J. Fleming purchased a plot of land from the family of Luis Peralta at the foot of what is now Gilman Street in Berkeley.

Politicians carved Alameda County from Contra Costa and Santa Clara counties in 1853. Alvarado was chosen as the first county seat, but was soon supplanted by San Leandro. The county seat followed a northward progression, settling first in the town of Brooklyn and then in Oakland, where it remains today.

In 1866 scholars and their supporters found a site for the College of California, which had been operating on a shoestring in Oakland. They named the place Berkeley to honor George Berkeley, a philosopher and the bishop of Cloyne in Ireland, who had come to America earlier in the century to establish universities.

With the arrival of the transcontinental railroad in 1869, travel became faster, easier, and less expensive. Merchants could now ship goods to the East without worrying about the perilous and often costly journey by boat around Cape Horn. Like the gold rush twenty years earlier, the train brought more people to the region—people who would lay the foundation for the East Bay in the twentieth century.

William Rust opened a blacksmith shop in 1888 in a town that would bear his name for a time; this was the foundation for the town of El Cerrito. Rust later erected a hardware store, where the town's first post office was established in 1909.

In 1890 the Piedmont Cable Company began transporting residents to that part of the city of Oakland. Piedmonters declared their independence from Oakland on January 30, 1907, and became a curiosity: a city completely surrounded by a city.

The city of Ocean View came into existence in 1908. The following year, voters changed the name of their city, primarily to distinguish it from another Ocean View right next door that had become a part of Berkeley. They voted to name the town Albany to honor the birthplace of their first mayor, Frank Roberts.

Richmond and its "suburb," Point Richmond, lie on the peninsula separating San Pablo Bay from San Francisco Bay. Richmond was incorporated on August 7, 1905. The city of San Pablo came into existence on April 27, 1948, when its residents voted to create a city government, with J. H. Crawford as its first mayor.

We record a scant 228 years in this volume, but we cannot forget that humans have lived here for over 5,000 years. The Ohlones had hunted and gathered in the area since their arrival. Then Juan Baptiste de Anza's expedition came and changed their way of life forever. The Franciscans converted the natives to a new religion— they introduced them to a civilization that claimed their land, their beliefs, their health, and, too often, their lives. The Ohlone Cemetery on Washington Boulevard in Fremont bears silent witness to their presence here. Ohlone chief Tarino, who helped lay the cornerstone on the first mission chapel, lies in this sacred ground.

Today the East Bay presents a vibrant picture that is in sharp contrast with that of the early 1900s. Dirt roads and winding lanes have become interstate highways. The AC Transit system, BART, and the automobile have replaced local trains and streetcars. The Great San Francisco Earthquake and Fire of 1906 radically changed building codes: steel and concrete structures now stand in place of those made of wood. Technologies that its founders could scarcely have imagined are now the norm, putting today's East Bay on the cutting edge of progress.

The establishment of Mission San Jose on June 11, 1797, marks the earliest European presence in the East Bay. Father Fermin de Lausen dedicated the fourteenth mission along the El Camino Real to Saint Joseph and christened it La Mission del Gloriosisimo Patriarca Señor San Jose, a name that was later shortened to Mission San Jose. The Spaniards eventually extended their control over the surrounding territory and 24,000 head of valuable cattle provided hides, tallow, and sustenance for the newcomers. The mission's permanent adobe church was dedicated on April 22, 1809. This photo was taken in 1867, a year before a massive earthquake rendered the adobe uninhabitable.

After the 1868 earthquake, members of the parish replaced the damaged adobe structure with a wooden French Gothic Revival–style church. The Native Sons and Daughters of the Golden West worked to save and restore the surviving portions of the mission; they converted it into a museum, which is set in gracious surroundings of flowers and palm trees. After extensive excavations by archaeologists, construction began in 1982 on this replica of the 1809 adobe church. It was completed and rededicated on June 11, 1985.

In 1841 José de Jesus Vallejo established a flour mill near this spot. He laid out the town with his son Plutarco and named it Vallejo Mills. The Central Pacific Railroad arrived in 1869, and its line split nearby: one line carried freight and passengers to Oakland, the other branch took trains to San Jose. Later, in 1883, the railroad established a new town and named it Niles for one of its major stockholders, Judge Addison C. Niles. This photo shows the west side of Main Street in Niles after the turn of the twentieth century, just as Gilbert M. "Bronco Billy" Anderson might have seen it when he arrived in 1912. Niles was the site of Essanay Studios, which filmed 375 twelve-minute movies featuring Anderson.

Charlie Chaplin and Wallace Beery also worked at the studios. In 1915 the studio filmed one of Chaplin's classics, *The Tramp*; a year later it closed its doors and moved to Hollywood. A brick building has replaced the wooden Masonic Hall, which the Masons moved elsewhere in the town. Today's Main Street offers a stop just off Mission Boulevard for anyone shopping for antiques, looking for a respite for a quiet lunch or dinner, or just wishing to step back in time. The Niles Canyon Railway still runs today as a living history museum.

Five Corners describes the intersection of five roads at one point in Fremont's Irvington district. The residents originally named their town Irving, but a printer at the railroad's press heard otherwise. When the railroad printed brochures identifying the town as Irvington, the name stuck. Three of the streets that merge into Five Corners also had other names when this photo, which captures a Fourth of July celebration early in the twentieth century, was taken: San Jose and the Irvington-Centerville roads now form Fremont Boulevard and Mission Road has become Washington Boulevard. Bay and Union streets have kept their original names.

Five Corners presents a much different story today. When the automobile appeared on the scene, San Jose Road became one of California's main north-south highways. Traffic increased dramatically at this intersection and Five Corners became the site of an alarming number of accidents. In 1917, after a head-on collision took the life of a young Irvington man, the chamber of commerce installed a monument to separate the traffic. Traffic lights have since replaced the monument as the primary means of controlling traffic, while a steady procession of cars has supplanted the crowds seen in the earlier photo.

This is a view looking north at the Goodell Block on B Street from Main Street in Hayward. The Holmes Market stood here, and nearby, at 1015 B Street, one could stop by Madsen's Variety Store for sundries. The block is named for George A. Goodell, who arrived in Hayward in 1865 and opened the town's first harness store on B Street. Active in the town's politics, he served as a town trustee and as a director of the Lone Tree Cemetery; he graciously offered the use of his hall for community meetings.

In 1927, the Greek Revival–style Bank of America Building replaced the Colonial Revival–style wooden building that once stood at the corner. The turn-of-the-century City Beautiful movement had a major influence on the design, planning, and management of American cities from New York to San Francisco. Its effects are still felt today and include monumental but low-lying buildings like the Bank of America here. The street still serves Hayward's needs with its many stores and restaurants. Downtown Hayward's pleasant blend of old and new makes the city attractive to shoppers and diners from the entire region.

Eggert's Blacksmith Shop stood on Main Street between B and C streets. Henry Eggert Sr. was an immigrant who arrived from Germany in the 1870s. At first Eggert worked for Hayward blacksmith Joe Rivers, but in 1878 he bought Rivers out. Eggert ran a full-service shop: he shod horses, repaired wagons, fabricated metal parts, and built wagons and carriages. The shop stood until just after World War I, when Eggert realized that the automobile could make his profession obsolete.

The Green Shutter Plaza graces the block that once echoed with the sounds of Henry Eggert's hammer and anvil. In 1918 the Eggert family replaced the blacksmith shop with a building that at first housed stores on the ground floor and offices upstairs. In 1926, with the demise of the Hayward Hotel, the need to accommodate travelers grew. So Henry's sons, Herman and Henry Jr., turned the upstairs floor into a hotel. They couldn't think of a name for their new hostelry until Henry Jr. found some green shutters on the street in San Francisco. When he learned that they were for sale, he purchased them and thus came up with the name for their new hotel. The Wilbur Market and the telephone exchange once stood just across the street. Today's Green Shutter Plaza includes shops and the hotel.

In 1852, Don Guillermo Castro offered William Hayward forty acres of land in present-day downtown Hayward. The enterprising Hayward opened a general trading store, which became a stagecoach stop, a post office, and a hotel. Hayward later became a postmaster, a justice of the peace, a county supervisor, and the roadmaster for Eden Township. Hayward and his second wife, Rachel, established Hayward's Hotel, one of the area's finest resorts. Sadly, the hotel suffered the fate of many early wooden structures: it burned down in 1926.

Although Don Castro referred to what is now downtown Hayward as "San Lorenzo," many called the town "Hayward's Place" or "Hayward's" because of the famous Hayward's Hotel. When the post office was established in 1860, a clerical error gave the town the official name of "Haywood." Haywood was incorporated in 1876 as the "Town of Haywards," with a total population of 1,100. In 1894, the superfluous "s" was dropped and on September 18, 1928, the status of the community was changed to the "City of Hayward." The site of the hotel at the intersection of B and Main streets is now home to commercial ventures. A plaque on the brick building in the distance reminds us that the Hayward family once lived here.

A streetcar can be seen approaching in the distance in this 1890 photo of Castro Street. The street was home to Hayward's first fire station, seen here with the tower that housed the station's warning bell in the days before sirens. The fire station also served as a meeting place for the town council. In 1913 the station was moved to D and Atherton streets. The city then relocated the fire station in 1997 to a site at C and Main streets. Presently, a total of nine fire stations serve the citizens of Hayward.

This block, just around the corner from Hayward's new city hall, has changed over the years to accommodate the need for downtown parking. Castro Street has become Mission Boulevard, the main thoroughfare that runs from north to south through the area. In San Leandro, Mission Boulevard becomes East Fourteenth Street and in East Oakland it changes its name to International Boulevard. Only one building survives from the turn of the last century, the 1906, double-fronted dwelling to the left of the picture, built by Joseph Prioste, who arrived in Hayward in 1900. He ran a general store from the ground floor premises and his family still owns the building today.

The columns of the Bank of Italy Building grace the corner of B Street and Mission Boulevard in Hayward. The Farmers and Merchants Bank built this Greek Revival–style building in 1911. It presents a more graceful example of the Greek Revival style than that seen in the 1927 Bank of America Building at B and Main streets. In 1921, the Bank of Italy purchased the Farmers and Merchants Bank and moved in. The Bank of Italy, which was succeeded by the Bank of America, helped bring stability to the region after the Great San Francisco Earthquake and Fire of 1906. Despite the name, the trembler affected a wide area that included Hayward.

Modern renovations can scarcely disguise the grace of the old Bank of Italy Building.
The Bank of Italy occupied the structure until 1927, when it became the Bank of
America and moved to B and Main streets. The original building was converted into
stores. Many old-time Hayward residents will remember Blank's, the clothing store
that moved into the building. The Hayward Theater stood just across the street.
Other stores have replaced those seen in the earlier photo as demands have changed
over the years.

Above: In 1881, Henry A. Thomford opened what was probably the first business in Castro Valley. Known as the Exchange, it was located on the corner of Grove Way and Redwood Road. Thomford figured that both the teamsters who drove on the dusty Dublin Road from Livermore Valley and their horses would want a drink on their way to and from the stockyards and markets in Hayward, or beyond to San Francisco. After the horses were watered at his troughs, the drivers would head into the saloon for a schooner of beer. Thomford also offered cheese, pickles, and fresh German sausages prepared by his wife. He filled the Exchange's rooms with oddities that included a three-headed chicken preserved in a jar.

Right: The First Presbyterian Church now stands on the site, not far from what might be considered Castro Valley's downtown. In the 1930s the Castro Valley Gardens, an Italian-style restaurant, occupied this spot. Historically, Castro Valley has been known for its chicken farming and is considered part of the East Bay's "farming bowl" that stretches from Alameda's Bay Farm Island to Fremont. Castro Valley was second only to Petaluma in Marin County for egg production during World War II. It remains unincorporated to Alameda County and has been growing rapidly as one of the up-and-coming areas of the East Bay.

In its heyday the Estudillo House advertised "private dining rooms, fine private picnic grounds, French dinners served in the best style at all hours, day or night—55 minutes to San Francisco." Built in 1855, the hotel, stage, and streetcar stop belonged to the Estudillo family and was operated under a succession of proprietors until 1918. This photo was taken before a bicycle race through San Leandro sometime between 1892 and 1898. The building suffered some damage in the 1868 earthquake that destroyed the county courthouse. Estudillo House was the center of community and politics in the county for sixty years.

The building remained at 201 San Lorenzo Avenue until 1929, when the Godchaux Building replaced it. Today, the southwest corner of Davis and Washington streets continues to be part of the heart of downtown San Leandro, a friendly and diverse city with a colorful heritage and numerous cultural amenities, including a 450-berth marina. The city has also become famous for its delicious cherries. In 1909, San Leandro held its first Cherry Festival, an event that is still celebrated today.

A covered bridge, a rarity on the West Coast, crossed San Leandro Creek at Fourteenth Street. This bridge was built in 1876, replacing one built in 1854. A third bridge dates to 1901. The Oakland, San Leandro & Haywards Electric Railway line ran on the trestle seen to the left, and the rail line offered a stop at the Estudillo House. The bridge served as an important traffic link for many years, dating back to the time of the Mexican landholders.

Root Park, a state historical landmark, stands today near the intersection of San Leandro Creek and East Fourteenth Street. The site marks the line between two land grants, the San Antonio Grant to Luis Peralta and the San Leandro Grant to José Joaquin Estudillo. The park also features a monument to the Portuguese immigrants, a gift to the city from the Uniao Portuguese do Estado da California. The statue celebrates the Portuguese influence on San Leandro; many Portuguese immigrants to the West Coast originated from the Azores.

San Leandro served as Alameda's county seat after a contentious political battle between Horace Carpentier of Oakland and those who favored the existing seat at Alvarado. San Leandro, a popular favorite, was chosen as a compromise. In 1855, Don Estudillo's sons-in-law, sea captain William H. Davis and John B. Ward, acquired a piece of land for a new courthouse and permission to design a town. In all, four of the Mexican landowner's daughters would marry Americans who shared in the business dealings and holdings of the family. Erected in 1856, this courthouse served Alameda County until 1873.

The county courthouse was destroyed by a temblor on October 12, 1868, a fate that was predicted in an 1861 issue of the *Alameda County Gazette*. Deputy County Clerk J. W. Josselyn died when the stone cornice of the building fell and crushed him. The jailer lost his keys in the earthquake and fearful prisoners had to be freed through a window. The embarrassment and losses caused by this event fueled Horace Carpentier's efforts to have the county seat moved to Oakland. Continued rapid population growth and Oakland's designation as the new terminus of the Central Pacific's transcontinental rail line contributed to Carpentier getting his way in 1872. The remains of the courthouse were at first refurbished and then in 1880 were used for St. Mary's School. The site is now occupied by Saint Leander's Church.

The main traffic corridor of Haywards Road and the location of Estudillo House, the covered bridge, and other civic structures and housing in growing San Leandro made placement of the downtown obvious. San Leandro Plaza served as a ceremonial street and as a meeting place in front of many of the businesses. In the 1880s, places like O. J. Lynch's pharmacy, James Doris's blacksmith shop, the J. A. Holmgren Dry Goods and Grocery Store, Gorman's Saloon, and the Odd Fellows Building all fronted the plaza. The plaza was also an ideal location for a streetcar stop. This photograph was taken on May 7, 1892, the day the Oakland, San Leandro & Haywards Electric Railway line held its opening-day celebration at the plaza. Parades, races, and other outdoor events would regularly take place here.

Today, San Leandro's downtown has grown to include several major office buildings. Access to the Bay Area Rapid Transit system (BART) has allowed for widespread commercial growth in the area around the plaza. Once a hub for streetcar commuter rail, the area that comprises the San Leandro Plaza now benefits from similar rail services just a few blocks away. Despite the plaza's new appearance, San Leandro's industrious spirit and entrepreneurship is the one thing that hasn't changed. Many businesses, both corporate and smaller operations, continue to thrive.

Public Library, San Leandro.

Fifty or sixty books collected through the efforts of O. J. Lynch in his pharmacy were the only "library" in San Leandro at first. Later, a room would be set aside in the Gorman Building at 305 Hayward Avenue. A Carnegie Foundation grant of $10,000 was approved in December 1907, and another $2,000 a year later, for erecting a library in San Leandro. The city contributed the maintenance costs and residents provided the furnishings. San Leandro's Carnegie Library was one of many in the East Bay: Oakland, Alameda, and Richmond also had libraries donated to them through the Carnegie Foundation. The Carnegie Library, which was completed in 1909, served the city until 1961, when the new Community Library Center was built.

The San Leandro Library has gone through another significant transformation
recently; its renovation and reconstruction have made it one of the newest
and most advanced public libraries in the East Bay. The new facility offers
free computer use, computer training classes, a history room that re-creates
the interior of the original Carnegie Library in the Classical Revival style,
and even a café and gift shop.

This look down East Fourteenth Street in the 1930s shows commercial development in the area south of what would become the civic center. The trees in the distance mark San Leandro Creek and the covered bridge. Root Park and the Portuguese immigrant monument are on the far side of the creek. The building with the conical tower marks the intersection of Davis and East Fourteenth streets; one block to the right stands the San Leandro library. The left side of East Fourteenth is San Leandro Plaza.

This street's presence in the community remains almost the same today. Just past the trees in the distance, the town hall and a beautiful civic center keep the area vibrant. East Fourteenth Street's many diverse businesses stretch from Oakland through San Leandro to Hayward, and include San Leandro's Bay Fair Mall. Once car culture got a grip on the East Bay, East Fourteenth Street south of Oakland became a common place to cruise. In the 1960s drive-in theaters and the Hells Angels came to East Fourteenth Street.

The Alaska Packers Association was incorporated in 1893. In all, twenty-three canneries would eventually belong to the association. The fleet of huge square-rigger ships spent the winters docked on the north shore of Alameda near Grand Street. Traversing the Pacific from the Golden Gate to the shores of Alaska, these fishing vessels would return each fall and store salmon in their holds until the canneries demanded more. The association marketed its salmon under the brand name Argo. The *Star of Alaska*, an Alaska Packer ship that has been restored to her launch name, *Balclutha*, still sails the San Francisco Bay on special occasions.

At the foot of Grand Street, Grand Marina keeps its slips full and active today, as Alameda continues to serve as the most important hub for recreational boating in the Bay Area. The city contains no fewer than three major boating-supply warehouses, many yacht clubs and marinas, yacht brokers, boatbuilders, sailmakers, riggers, woodworkers, and other specialized boating industries. Across the estuary, condos off Oakland's historic Jack London Square offer new views of the waterway. Many of writer Jack London's journeys would begin and end at Oakland's waterfront bar, Heinhold's First and Last Chance Saloon.

The intersection of Park Street and Santa Clara Avenue has long been considered the center of Alameda. This picture was taken in 1942, when Alameda bustled with wartime industry. Prior to World War II, the Bay Area hadn't considered its military options and so an organization was created between the military and local captains of industry to prepare the region. The Metropolitan Defense Committee had hundreds of acres of landfill added to Alameda's west end for use as a Navy base. Expeditions launched from Alameda's base during World War II included the 1942 raid on Tokyo led by Colonel Jimmy H. Doolittle.

Park Street is the main thoroughfare into downtown Alameda today. Park Street adjoins the civic center of the city, with the city hall, police station, Alameda High School, the Elks Lodge, and the new library all within a block of this intersection. Park Street's longest-standing businesses include the Boniere Bakery, originally a candy shop founded in 1877; Cavanaugh Motors, a Chrysler dealer dating from 1918; and Ole's Waffle Shop, a popular diner that opened in the 1920s.

The First Presbyterian Church opened its doors in 1904 at the corner of Chestnut Street and Santa Clara Avenue. Reverend Brush, the first clergyman at the church, traveled to Europe in 1902 when First Presbyterian was still located at Versailles and Central avenues. The reverend was impressed by the stained glass he saw in Italy—all the stained glass that can be seen in the church today was imported as a result. Some of the lumber at an earlier church, built in 1869, was saved and reused in this building.

Today the church shares its space with the Korean Presbyterian Church and a day-care center. The church, which recently celebrated its centennial, was added to the National Register of Historic Places in 1980. A recent renovation got the building painted, the windows cleaned, and the steps repaired. Various community groups use the space, including the Alameda Architectural Preservation Society and Boy Scout Troop 2. Members at First Presbyterian also helped start Alameda's Meals on Wheels program, which serves seniors and invalids in the community.

Prior to the 1906 earthquake, Alameda City Hall featured a 120-foot-tall bell tower that was partially dislodged on that fateful day in April 1906. This 1896 structure was one of the few buildings in Alameda that was damaged by the quake. It replaced the city's original city hall at Park Street and Webb Avenue, which also housed the police and fire departments and the city jail. Christ Episcopal Church previously stood on this site before being moved to the corner of Grand Street and Santa Clara Avenue.

City Hall continues to operate under the watchful eye of the mayor of Alameda, whose office is across Oak Street in the Times-Star Building. The top of City Hall's tower was removed immediately after the 1906 earthquake, and the remainder of the bell tower was finally removed in 1937, when it was determined structurally unsafe. Across Santa Clara Avenue, Alameda's own Carnegie Library opened in 1903 and recently underwent an earthquake retrofit. Alameda City Hall is today listed on the National Register of Historic Places.

In this photo of Park Street looking south to Alameda Avenue in 1905, one can see the watershed of two different forms of transportation. Even though the automobile has arrived, horses and buggies were still in wide use at this time. Just past the Alameda Avenue intersection, the Old Masonic Temple, built in 1891 at 1327–31 Park Street, towers above its neighbors. Both telegraph and telephone were in use, as evidenced by the different wire poles. This shot is looking toward the south shore of the island.

Today Park Street has already felt the beginnings of revitalization through the efforts of John Knowles, a property owner who completely updated and upgraded the building that fronts the corner of Central Avenue and Park Street. By attracting high-profile tenants to locate here, the district has been drawing a more varied clientele. The Old Masonic Temple now houses a popular local café, while the New Masonic Temple, built in 1927, is located next door.

CHESTNUT STREET STATION AND ELECTRIC TRAIN
ALAMEDA, CALIFORNIA.
1021A.

Chestnut Street's first major development, the Notre Dame Academy for Girls, opened in 1881; the small Catholic sanctuary of St. Joseph Church on Santa Clara Avenue was moved to the site in that same year. Once the streetcar arrived, prolific Alameda architect Joseph A. Leonard began building a significant residential area nearby. "Leonardville" would continue construction until 1896. The first of the seventy residences Leonard built in 1889 stood on Chestnut and Lafayette streets, adjoining this station. Leonard also designed the kiosk seen here.

Another of Alameda's small shopping districts, Chestnut Street Station offers locals a wide array of services, including several stores and restaurants. St. Joseph Notre Dame High School is only half a block away; the St. Joseph's Basilica was erected on the campus in 1921. The districts around where streetcar stations once resided give Alameda its unique historic feel and a diverse sampling of commercial architecture.

Croll's Hotel and Restaurant was erected in 1879. Originally known as the Britt Hotel, it was built by Patrick Britt, whose farm at the foot of Webster was purchased for development as the Long Branch Baths. Called Neptune Beach in the 1920s and 1930s, this popular bathing resort on San Francisco Bay was often referred to as the "Coney Island of the West Coast." Britt's land sold for $6,000; with this money he built Webster Street's first hotel, which adjoined the Southern Pacific tracks along Central Avenue. The Croll family would eventually acquire and rename the building.

Since the closure of the Naval Air Station in Alameda, Webster Street's commercial district has had to adapt. Once a place of dry cleaners, bars, and barber shops, the clientele in the area has changed. Many long-standing businesses continue to thrive, but Croll's was one of the casualties of fewer drinking sailors during and after World War II. Restaurants and bars have had trouble staying open at this location, and today a real estate company occupies the downstairs office. The building is listed on the National Register of Historic Places.

Park Street and Central Avenue looking north in 1905 shows the Bank of Alameda Building, which still stands today, in the right foreground. The Library Block, the large building on the left, was constructed in 1896 and housed the original public library until the Carnegie Library was completed in 1903. The Artesian Water Works Building of 1881 looms over the bank at right. The Water Works Building took a year to build—twenty-five tons of iron bars were used to support a backup reservoir of 250,000 gallons on the building's fourth floor.

Park Street still enjoys plenty of commercial hustle and bustle as Alameda enters an era of renaissance. Since the Alameda Naval Air Station closed its doors in the late 1990s, Alameda's median income has increased dramatically. Many companies have an interest in tapping into this new and growing market and talk of redeveloping the mostly vacant base has spurred growth all over the island, including on Park Street. Merchants in the district look forward to the construction of a seven-screen cinema and a large parking garage a block away from this intersection.

The 1896 Encinal Hotel, at the corner of Encinal Avenue and High Street, housed visitors to the High Street Station. The Oakland–Alameda rail line ran through town on a circuit that linked to the "Alameda mole," a streetcar connection to the ferry to San Francisco. The various streetcar stations in town gave rise to much vibrant commercial architecture. Hotels such as these were also used to house prospective real-estate investors and transients. It is said that during the 1940s and 1950s, the building served as a brothel and bar for golfers retiring after a round at the course on Alameda's Bay Farm Island. The "19th Hole" sign remains to this day.

Today the building, after many remodels, contains apartments above the ground-level storefronts. A computer repair shop and the Alameda School of Music are the current tenants, and a third commercial space is unoccupied. The area has retained the name High Street Station through the efforts of the Greater Alameda Business Association and still features a strong commercial neighborhood despite the absence of the trains. A church group is said to be opening a teen-run coffee shop on this corner after the new doors and windows are installed.

Alameda High School nears completion in January 1926. The original structure, built in 1903, needed expansion. Using the Classic Revival style of architecture on a grand scale, a wing of the building faces the entire 2200 block of Central Avenue. Sports teams at the school actually took the Hornets as their mascot before Alameda's historic aircraft carrier, the USS *Hornet*, was constructed. The famous carrier served in the Doolittle raid during World War II; the second *Hornet*, currently a floating museum in Alameda, recovered the Apollo 13 spacecraft after its flight to the moon.

Today, Alameda High School's 1,700 students enjoy the campus, which takes up an entire block bounded by Central and Encinal avenues and Oak and Walnut streets. With a tradition dating back to 1875, Alameda High School's most famous student is probably Jim Morrison, lead singer for the Doors. The various structures associated with the campus include the Alameda Unified School District offices, the Alameda Recreation and Parks Department, the Alameda Adult School, the Alameda Civic Light Opera, and the interim site of the Alameda Free Library.

The 1874 River and Harbor Act called for a 400-foot-wide, mile-long channel to be cut through the neck of the Alameda Peninsula to connect the Alameda Estuary with San Leandro Bay. This photo dates to 1890. The Army Corps of Engineers dredged the estuary and a tidal basin as far as where Coast Guard Island is today. Two channels were cut from either end of the estuary toward the center. The original vision for the area included a dam at the San Leandro Bay that would open and close with the tides to direct currents through the man-made channel. As the tide flooded out of the estuary, the water would scour the silt and defeat the need for regular dredging.

It was decided in the 1920s that the dam would not work the way it was intended and so construction never got started. The fact that Alameda is an island today could be considered a big government boondoggle. Taxpayers' dollars went to waste to complete the estuary and cut Alameda off and yet the channel still needs regular dredging. The estuary serves as a highway for boat traffic with three drawbridges crossing it. Shipping continues at the Port of Oakland, a very important source of trade for the West Coast. Ferry services run between Alameda, Oakland, San Francisco, Tiburon, and a few other points on the bay. A water taxi shuttles people back and forth across the estuary—between Mariner Square in Alameda and Jack London Square in Oakland. The Coast Guard runs a base on Coast Guard Island, created in 1913 as part of the initial dredging program.

Prior to the construction of the Posey Tube, the Webster and Harrison street bridges provided trains and cars a means of travel across the estuary. These connections to the West End gave rise to Webster Street as the "other downtown." Soon after the turn of the century, local officials suggested the idea of a tunnel under the estuary to ease car and shipping traffic. By 1928 the tunnels became a reality after a five-year construction phase by California Bridge and Tunnel Company. George A. Posey, chief engineer and one of the county supervisors who made the project possible, gave his name to the new tunnel.

The Posey Tube now provides a necessary link between Alameda and Oakland. The tube underwent earthquake retrofitting, which was completed in early 2004. Oakland's Chinatown politicians and Alameda officials recently had a disagreement about traffic impact on the tube after the redevelopment of the vacant Naval Air Station property is completed. During World War II, the tube clogged up with traffic each morning and evening as workers showed up for work at the base. Residents today claim that similar traffic patterns will develop once new homes, businesses, and recreational areas (including a championship golf course and the Bay Trail, which is to circumscribe the entire San Francisco Bay) are completed. The factory where Skippy peanut butter was first made was on Webster Street, just across from the tube. Alameda has a long tradition of incubating new businesses, and Skippy flew the nest in the 1970s. Their factory was torn down in the 1990s.

Architect Albert Farr designed and built this unique combination of city hall and fire station in 1909. The city of Piedmont moved into the building at 120 Vista Avenue in 1910. To accommodate the fire department, Farr's original design included a bell tower and hose-drying apparatus. Farr also designed the nearby Piedmont Community Church and many homes in the city. The first fire engine purchased by the city in 1910 can be seen in the apparatus bay and also in the inset picture. In 1877 James Gamble bought 350 acres of land from Walter Blair. Gamble established the Piedmont Land Company and lent the community its name. Gamble's estate took up an entire city block near the city hall; the site is now a recreation center with a pool and tennis courts.

To accommodate a growing city government, the city of Piedmont added a second floor to its city hall. A modern, state-of-the-art fire department is still at home here; a siren has replaced the bell tower and the firefighters have new ways of drying their hoses. Incorporated in 1907, Piedmont is unique in the United States: it is the only city that is completely surrounded by another city—Oakland.

This Beaux Arts–style city hall reinforced Joseph S. Emery's declaration of independence. By 1896 his long-running battles with Alameda County over land taxes and with the city of Oakland over its failure to provide municipal services led to his incorporation of 185 acres bordering Oakland and Berkeley as Emeryville. W. H. Christie served as mayor, a position he held for more than thirty years. The citizens of the new town celebrated with bonfires in the streets and impromptu "jollification meetings." For seven years, until 1903 when the city hall was built, city leaders conducted business in two small rooms of the Commercial Union Hotel at the foot of Park Avenue. They decided that Park Avenue should be the civic center of Emeryville.

Emeryville's unique city hall served the city until 1971, when it moved into a new building. The city moved back in 1978 though. In 1989, the Loma Prieta Earthquake damaged the building and repairs were made in time for the city's centennial celebration in 1996. A 17,500-square-foot glass-and-steel wing was added to the original three-story, 7,500-square-foot structure.

The addition includes administrative offices and multipurpose areas. On June 9, 2001, the citizens of Emeryville celebrated the grand reopening of their historic city hall and civic center. There were no reports of any "jollification meetings" this time.

Emeryville has served the Bay Area as a thriving industrial town. The northern part of town was referred to as "Butchertown" for its stockyards and slaughterhouses. Orchards grew all along the entire East Bay. Canneries were started up to package and ship fruit to both national and international destinations. In 1919, the Western Cannery Company was built on Park Avenue, and the Virden Canning Company took over operations in 1927. When this photo was taken in the early 1920s, the factory employed 1,500 workers during peak periods.

Del Monte closed its plant in 1988 and now Pixar Studios occupies the cannery
site. Creators of the movies *Monsters, Inc.*, *A Bug's Life*, and *Toy Story*, the
company relocated its computer animation studio from Richmond, California,
to the former cannery site in 2000. The studio designed its offices as a corporate
campus, which currently includes 150,000 square feet of office space and a 50,000-
square-foot screening theater. Pixar sees a bright future in Emeryville: the company
is planning to construct three new buildings totaling 600,000 square feet.

The Fabiola Hospital in Oakland owes its existence to the philanthropy of Catherine Mix Kirkham. She witnessed a carriage accident in downtown Oakland and was horrified to learn that the victim would be transported to San Leandro, which was the nearest public hospital at the time. She prevailed upon her husband, Brevet Brigadier General Ralph Kirkham, and his wealthy capitalist friends to donate money to establish a hospital in Oakland. A hospital and dispensary were maintained in various places until 1888, when the association built this permanent Queen Anne–style building at what is now Broadway and MacArthur Boulevard. The hospital was named for Saint Fabiola, a fourth-century woman credited with opening the first public hospital in Europe.

The Kaiser Permanente Medical Care Program dedicated its Oakland hospital in 1942, the first in the chain of Henry J. Kaiser's hospitals. The Kaiser Permanente Medical Care Program began as Dr. Sidney A. Garfield's twelve-bed field hospital in the middle of the Mojave Desert in the 1930s. The small hospital served Henry J. Kaiser's Los Angeles Aqueduct workers. Kaiser Permanente has grown into America's largest nonprofit health-care organization; it serves more than eight million subscribers. Kaiser Hospital's campus, pictured here, still has a Fabiola Building in honor of Catherine Mix Kirkham and the first hospital on this site.

The bell that tolled for the dead and funereal urns decorate this entryway and define it as the gate to Oakland's Mountain View Cemetery. A glance through the passageway reveals the caretaker's home. The Main family mausoleum is visible through the arch at the far right. A Piedmont Railway Company streetcar and stonecutters' tools complete the picture. The cemetery was founded in 1863 and contains the finest examples of Victorian funerary architecture in the East Bay. Frederick Law Olmsted landscaped the cemetery's 220 acres. At the time, Olmsted was famous for his design of New York's Central Park. Mountain View was Olmsted's first private contract in what became a long and distinguished career.

The nineteenth-century gate has changed over the years to accommodate twentieth-century traffic. In the 1930s, the prominent architectural firm of Weeks and Day designed the Gothic Revival–style chapel that replaced the caretaker's home. More than 170,000 souls rest in Mountain View today. These include Charles Crocker of Central Pacific Railroad and Big Four fame, who rests beneath his impressive monument on the cemetery's Millionaire's Row. His neighbors were the movers and shakers who laid the foundation of the East Bay and beyond: Frances Shattuck, Edson Adams, George Pardee, and Samuel Merritt, to name just a few. A visit to Mountain View makes for an impressive journey into California history.

A 150-foot-tall stack spews smoke from the Consolidated Piedmont Cable Company's boilers at Twenty-fourth and Harrison streets in Oakland. On August 1, 1890, the company began operations from this cable-car power station and car barn. The passengers on the left are probably boarding one of the company's streetcars for Piedmont, while a buggy waits nearby. Coal was fed into the boilers to power the engines that drove the cables. The Piedmont Baths were built adjacent to the powerhouse to take advantage of the heat the boilers generated. On August 3, 1892, the railway company began service to Mountain View Cemetery; however, the powerhouse fell into disuse when the streetcar lines were electrified.

Memories of the cable company's powerhouse and the Piedmont Baths have faded. One almost always refers to the building today with the name of its second tenant, Cox Cadillac, which took over the building in 1923. The building has stood vacant since 1996. The city of Oakland has now promised that the "Cox Cadillac Project" will breathe new life into the site. A whole-foods store will occupy the front of the building, while the area at the rear of the building will be used for housing. Ground has already been broken; when this photograph was taken, the entire back of the building had already been demolished. The city has set a goal of both retail and homeowner occupancy by the fall of 2005.

The architectural firm of Oliver and Foulkes designed the Key Route Inn, a 180-room hotel that opened for business in March 1907. A diner could enjoy a full-course dinner in the hotel's banquet room for just a dollar at the time. The key seen behind the tower identified it with the Key Route System, the transportation grid that served most of the East Bay in its heyday. A passenger is seen here embarking on one of the system's electric streetcars. The buggies in the background define the early twentieth century in Oakland as a time when people still relied on the horse for transportation. Fire struck the Key Route Inn several times, but the construction of Grand Avenue brought on the wrecking ball. Edward Foulkes later went on to design Oakland's landmark Tribune Tower.

The Breuners Furniture Store replaced the Key Route Inn at Twenty-second and Broadway as one of two "emerald jewels": the other, the I. Magnin Building, stands just two blocks away. H. C. Capwell opened his department store at Twentieth and Broadway in 1927. This building serves as a reminder of the time when downtown Oakland was a shopping mecca. In the 1930s and 1940s, Oakland's uptown district began to attract fashionable apparel stores such as I. Magnin, the Gray Shop, Kushin's Shoes, Arden's, and Earl R. Lindburg. Some people express optimism about the twenty-first century as well. With the recent arrival of stores such as the Gap, downtown Oakland may reemerge as a destination for clothes shopping.

A horse-drawn streetcar makes its way across Lake Merritt on the Twelfth Street Dam on its way to East Oakland. Hiram Tubbs built a grand hotel in East Oakland in 1871. He needed a way to transport passengers from the Overland train station to his hotel, so he built the streetcar line. The Tubbs Hotel made a quiet respite for travelers away from the bustle of downtown Oakland. For years the "Tubbs Line" was the only way for passengers to get to destinations east of Lake Merritt. The fare was ten cents.

An AC Transit bus now travels the route downtown on Twelfth Street. The parking lot for the Henry J. Kaiser Convention Center lies in the direct foreground while high-rises and homes dot the landscape across the water. Lake Merritt is the largest tidal lake in the United States, as well as the nation's first waterfowl refuge. The lake is named for Samuel Merritt, an early Oakland mayor who played a large role in preserving the lake as it is today.

The intersection of Fruitvale Avenue and East Fourteenth Street bustles with urban activity. Fruitvale, named for the orchards and farms that provided the area with its business in the nineteenth century, was its own town until 1909, when it became a part of the city of Oakland. The bank building, the streetcar, and the people on the street lend vitality to a typical city street corner.

A palm tree marks the site of the old Citizen's Bank Building. Fruitvale is now a thriving district with a distinctive Hispanic flavor. Much has changed in the district as Oakland's Hispanic community has made Fruitvale its own. The Spanish Speaking Unity Council (SSUC) has helped revitalize the district with the Fruitvale Main Street Initiative and the Fruitvale Village project. The village, which celebrated its grand opening last May, houses the SSUC's headquarters, a public library, several community organizations, a computer technology center, a senior center, and forty-seven housing units. The developer of the project is the Fruitvale Development Corporation, a support corporation of the SSUC.

An automobile makes its way up Broadway as a horse and wagon approaches from Telegraph Avenue in this early twentieth-century photograph of the intersection of these streets. Nineteenth-century wooden structures abound, suggesting that this photo was taken before the 1906 earthquake. The structures include a three-story flatiron building. The Latham family would replace the oversized flagpole with a fountain; building regulations after the earthquake helped give downtown Oakland a fresher, more urban look. In just a few years skyscrapers would appear on the scene.

Wooden structures have disappeared and the Latham Fountain stands in its place, but one building dominates the intersection. Sometimes compared to a slice of wedding cake, the thirteen-story Federal Realty Building joined the downtown skyline in 1914. Its neo-Gothic style gave it the popular nickname of the "Cathedral Building." This building is one of the jewels in the Downtown Oakland Historic District, a National Historic Landmark that runs along Broadway from Eleventh to Seventh streets. The building itself is listed on the National Register of Historic Places.

Oakland's Beaux Arts city hall dominates the skyline in this 1915 photo taken from Alameda's United Engineering Works. A cluster of nearby skyscrapers joins the cityscape. The Alameda County Courthouse dome peeks out at the far left and the Hotel Oakland's twin Queen Anne–style towers can be seen on the right. Smoke from the boilers at the Piedmont Baths rises up from behind the hotel. The Webster Street Bridge crosses the Oakland Estuary next to the United Engineering Works, and a steam schooner lies moored at the Hogan Lumber Company on the Oakland side next to the bridge.

A much different, more vibrant Oakland presents itself today. City Hall stands tucked behind a modern high-rise in this photo taken from the silo in Alameda near the Posey Tube. Jack London Square lies along the Estuary on the Oakland side. The Webster Street Bridge is gone, as is the Harrison Street Bridge; the Posey and Webster tubes replaced them. Bridges were considered impediments to shipping traffic along the busy estuary. The Federal Building (left) and the Tribune Tower (right) stand out along the skyline. Close investigation will show the Hotel Oakland's twin towers are still there; it is now a home for senior citizens.

Children and adults frolic in a pond that once stood at the northeast corner of Tenth and Washington streets in the heart of what became downtown Oakland. Someone has labeled this photo in handwriting with the words "Our pond, northeast corner Tenth, Washington Street 1880." Washington Street continued east to meet Fourteenth Street, where Oakland City Hall then stood. Oakland's train station, the terminus for the transcontinental railroad, stood at Seventh Street and Broadway, four blocks in the other direction. Swan's Market later appeared just across the street.

The Oakland Convention Center now stands at the site of the old pond. This state-of-the-art center welcomes visitors and conventions from all over the world. The center also has a visitor's bureau that assists anyone with questions about visiting, living in, or even writing about Oakland. The Golden State Warriors, Oakland's professional basketball team, uses the center for practices.

Boaters and spectators enjoy a day at the Lake Merritt Boathouse. Lake Merritt is a 160-acre saltwater lagoon formed from a slough that was once part of the San Antonio Creek. The lake became a fashionable place to live as nineteenth-century developers—such as Samuel Merritt, for whom the lake is named—built lakeside homes for the wealthy. Only one of these homes remains today: the Camron-Stanford House, next to the boathouse. In 1870, Lake Merritt became an official wildlife refuge, providing sanctuary for migratory birds. Thousands of waterfowl winter here, attracted by the food and shelter available on the lake.

High-rises across the lake and a parking lot to accommodate the increased number of automobiles now frame the modern view of Lake Merritt. After serving as a boathouse, the building became offices for the city of Oakland. In 2004, funds became available to restore the boathouse. Lake Merritt remains an attraction to all in the East Bay; small boats and gondolas still ply its waters. The refuge is a National Historic Landmark.

J. W. Tucker and his son located their paint store at Fourteenth and Webster streets, just across from the narrow-gauge train station that stood at the present-day site of the Downtown Merchants Parking Garage. They pose here with their nineteenth-century status symbol: a horse and buggy. A train and its crew—in the right place at the right time—pose for the camera as well. Sign painter William J. Oakes shared the building with the Tuckers. Notice the paint barrels used as decoration on the building.

The automobile has replaced the train and a twentieth-century brick building stands where the Tuckers and Oakes plied their painting trades. The train tracks on Webster Street and the station across the street fell victim to progress. The automobile became so popular that twentieth-century merchants saw the need for a parking garage for their customers.

The Maclise Drugstore Building anchors the triangle, or gore, formed by San Pablo Avenue at Clay and Seventeenth Street. The three-story, neoclassical brick-and-stone commercial building dwarfs the adjacent buildings on San Pablo Avenue and the one on Jefferson Street. It is dwarfed in turn by Oakland's Beaux Arts–style city hall. Built between 1898 and 1899, the building may have been the keystone to plans for developing this corner. Seven years later, the First National Bank Building just down San Pablo rose to grace another downtown gore; in 1914 the Cathedral Building decorated a third.

The neoclassical building still stands as a modest reminder of nineteenth-century commercial architecture. The flatiron structure's golden glow shows that this jewel has been cared for over time. In 1989, the Loma Prieta Earthquake did extensive damage to the structure. The building underwent retrofitting in the early 1990s and now houses a law firm. It is a city of Oakland landmark.

Horses and automobiles mingle with the busy crowd at Oakland's first produce market at Eleventh and Harrison streets in 1904. As Oakland grew after the 1906 earthquake, homes began to encroach on this area. From around 1910 the market got a new set of neighbors as the blacksmiths and livery stable owners began to cater for a new industry: the horseless carriage. The boom experienced during the early 1920s drove up property values and so the produce market moved to a less populated area near the Oakland Estuary.

A commercial building has replaced the produce market. The building originally served Oakland's infant automobile industry. Until recently, the building had the signs of automobile manufacturers and repair shops in some of its windows, whispers of Oakland's first "Auto Row" that prospered along neighboring Twelfth Street until auto dealers moved to Broadway and sowed the seeds for Oakland's present-day Auto Row.

The Grand Lake Theatre takes center stage in this 1927 photograph of Grand Avenue. This theater was the first of three regal movie palaces built in Oakland. The Fox Oakland was built in 1928, followed by the Paramount in 1931. The Grand Lake Theatre, designed by the Reid brothers, opened its doors on March 6, 1926. A mighty Wurlitzer organ added spice to the films. In 1928, ice-cream maker William Dreyer formed a partnership with candy maker Joseph Edy and opened a shop just up Grand Avenue from the theater. Taking its name from Oakland's City Beautiful avenue, Dreyer's Grand Ice Cream was born.

The Grand Lake Theatre still draws moviegoers to its screens today—and audiences can still occasionally enjoy music from the mighty Wurlitzer's pipes. The theater now boasts four more intimate theaters with period design: one with Moorish decor and a second in Egyptian style. The nascent shopping district seen in the 1927 photo has grown into one of the most attractive districts in Oakland.

In 1922, *Oakland Tribune* publisher Joseph Russell Knowland commissioned architect Edward T. Foulkes to add a Renaissance Revival tower to his six-story Tribune Building. Foulkes's creation, which long dominated the skyline, would become the symbol for downtown Oakland. The building began life on Twelfth Street as Brueners Furniture Store in 1906. From July 5, 1922, until 1959, a radio tuned to KLX 910 on the dial would be airing a broadcast from the Tribune Tower.

The *Oakland Tribune* was forced to vacate its landmark office building and production plant after the 1989 Loma Prieta earthquake. Six years later, developer John Protopappas bought the building from a California bank for $350,000. In 2000, the Oakland Heritage Alliance honored Protopappas, owner of Madison Park Developers, architect Gary Guenther, and construction manager Judy Romann with a "Partnership in Preservation" award for their restoration of the tower. In 2001, after a hiatus of twelve years, the *Oakland Tribune* management and staff returned to what the OHA calls downtown Oakland's "keystone building." The $8 million renovation paved the way for the newspaper to move back in as a tenant.

Oakland's first city hall stood on Broadway between Third and Fourth streets, the second in Shattuck Hall at Eighth and Broadway. Then California's state legislature authorized Oakland to erect a permanent city hall. This Empire-style building with its mansard roof was completed in 1871. The building caught fire August 25, 1877. Unfortunately, the fire bell was in the burning building's tower and so the fire department arrived too late. The city offered a $1,000 reward for the arrest and conviction of the "incendiary who fired building," but the culprit was never caught.

The replacement city hall—number four in the sequence—survived until 1913, when the present structure replaced it. As the first skyscraper city hall building, Oakland's eighteen-story Beaux Arts city hall once stood as the tallest building west of the Mississippi. The jail on one of the top floors helped add to its impressive height. In 1911, the year construction began, Oakland's beloved mayor, Frank Mott, got married and Oaklanders dubbed the new building "Mayor Mott's Wedding Cake." This National Historic Landmark has a three-story podium, a ten-story office tower, and a two-story clock tower base that supports an ornamental clock tower ninety-two feet tall.

This impressive Queen Anne–style structure housed the Altenheim—a senior citizens' home—in Oakland's Dimond District. Oakland's German community had struck deep roots in the surrounding area and purchased the property in 1891 for $7,500. The following year they raised $37,000 for the building. On May 20, 1894, the first residents moved in. They paid $2,000 each for life care. In July 1908 the building was destroyed by fire, but thankfully there were no injuries or fatalities. A new facility was ready for occupancy in 1909.

The German community replaced the building with this Colonial Revival jewel. Sadly, the facility closed in 2002, as it was no longer profitable to run the aging full-service facility. The Citizens Housing Corporation has proposed a senior housing project on the site. The group hopes to build sixty-seven low-income apartments for seniors in its first phase of development. The developers promise a senior housing project that will suit this historic building and its surrounding landscape.

One can see the history of the railroad line that served Oakland at the Seventh Street Station in this photo. The monogram "CPR" on the pediment at top stands for Central Pacific Railroad; below, the "S. P." stands for Southern Pacific. The Central Pacific operated services until 1885, when the Southern Pacific took control. The last train ran on these tracks on March 21, 1941, when the Interurban Electric Railway abandoned the service. Oakland's first railway station (inset) stood at the same spot. Service began September 2, 1863, when engineer James Batchelder and his locomotive pulled three railcars to the ferry service on San Francisco Bay. The Central Pacific's first transcontinental service to Oakland and San Francisco arrived here on November 8, 1869.

Urban renewal has put a new face on Seventh Street, but the echo of
Southern Pacific's Seventh Street Station remains. Many Oaklanders
remember this as the site of the long-standing store Mi Rancho. The
store is gone, replaced by a pair of bail-bond agencies, conveniently
located near the Oakland Police Department, whose headquarters stand
just across the street.

The ferry *Garden City* takes on cargo and passengers at the busy Oakland wharf at the foot of Broadway. The coming of the railroad in 1863, with its wharf directly on San Francisco Bay, gave Oaklanders a choice between taking a ferry here or at the end of Seventh Street after riding the train to the bay. Ferries that picked up passengers at the foot of Broadway were said to be on the Creek Route to distinguish them from the ones that stopped on the bay. A three-masted schooner also lies at the pier, likely delivering lumber from the North Coast.

Author Jack London spent considerable time on the Oakland Estuary, on San Francisco Bay, and at the nearby Heinhold's First and Last Chance Saloon. Jack London Square at the foot of Broadway honors his presence in the city. London's statue stands at the foot of Broadway today as a reminder that he is very much a part of Oakland's history. Jack London Square is now a vibrant part of Oakland with restaurants, shops, and a hotel.

James H. Latham came to San Francisco in 1869 from Virginia City, Nevada, where he had worked as a bank representative for Wells Fargo. After his arrival, he enjoyed a successful career with a brokerage firm. He built this Empire-style residence with its signature Mansard roof on Oakland's Jackson Street for his wife, Henrietta, and their family. The home looked over Lake Merritt. The family's legacy, the Latham Foundation for the Promotion of Humane Education, still carries on their work: teaching others about the humane treatment of animals. James and Henrietta's children erected the Latham Memorial Fountain in 1913 to honor their parents. The fountain still stands in front of the Cathedral Building in downtown Oakland.

The Lathams' stately home was demolished around 1957. The neighborhood of grand, exclusive estates for the wealthy along the shores of Lake Merritt has given way to apartment buildings. Memory of the Lathams remained fresh in the 1950s and into the 1960s, however. Those who grew up in the area at this time may remember *The Brother Buzz Show* that the Latham Foundation sponsored. The main character, Brother Buzz, visited petting zoos and other locations featuring animals, and talked to children about treating all creatures with consideration and kindness.

The University of California traces its roots to this site in Oakland, the College of California. It opened in 1860; its curriculum emphasized the classics. On March 23, 1868, it merged with the Agricultural, Mining, and Mechanical Arts College to become the University of California. The new campus was four miles north, on a site they called Berkeley. Seen in the inset is the Fourth and Franklin Street Station (located behind the college and to the left), where a train bound for Alameda prepares for its trip down Webster Street. The Southern Pacific Railroad, which acquired the station from the narrow-gauge South Pacific Coast Rail Road in 1887, made renovations in 1923 to suit standard-gauge trains.

The Downtown Merchants Association erected a two-story parking garage at the birthplace of the University of California and the old train station. A plaque on the garage wall at Thirteenth and Franklin, where this photo was taken, commemorates the university's beginnings.

The transcontinental railroad arrived in Oakland in 1869. The center of population followed; it shifted from the county's agricultural south to Oakland in the north. As a result, Oakland rose to prominence. Six years later, in 1875, Alameda County, California's second most populous county, got a courthouse that showed its new status to the world. The county hired leading architects John and Thomas Newsom to design a Renaissance Revival jewel. Their finished product, a domed cathedral to display the wealth of Oakland and Alameda County, rose up on Washington Square on Broadway between Fourth and Fifth streets.

Tastes change with the times. As early as 1933, a call went out to condemn the county's antiquated courthouse. A modern courthouse sprang up on the shores of Lake Merritt. The old courthouse survived only another seventeen years. It fell to the wrecking ball in 1950; the county replaced it with this boxlike structure that still functions as offices.

Architect John Galen Howard—who designed much of the UC Berkeley campus, including the Sather Tower—fashioned this nine-foot-high, double-tiered fountain on Marin Circle to celebrate Berkeley's Northbrae neighborhood. Arthur Putman sculpted the bear cubs to symbolize the state of California and the university, whose mascot is the Golden Bear. Howard also designed the stone pillars that mark the neighborhood's streets, the entrance pillars on the Alameda, as well as a real-estate office and train station that no longer stand.

A replica of Howard and Putnam's creation stands at the intersection today. A runaway truck destroyed the fountain in 1958. The circle remained without its signature fountain for almost forty years. Then, in 1993, residents formed Friends of the Fountain and raised $175,000. Sculptor Sarita White faithfully re-created Putnam's bear cubs, and in 1996 a community celebration welcomed the new fountain to the circle.

2872 – City Hall, Berkeley, California.

Architects John Bakewell and Arthur Brown designed and built this handsome Beaux Arts city hall for Berkeley. The building was completed in 1909. Both men had graduated from UC Berkeley in the 1890s. They modeled the structure after the city hall in Tours, France. They intended for the building's spire to support clocks, but the city never purchased them. Bakewell and Brown also designed San Francisco City Hall and buildings on the UC Berkeley campus. After they dissolved their partnership in 1928, Brown designed the San Francisco landmark Coit Tower.

Old City Hall served the Berkeley city government until 1977; city council meetings are still held here. The building now houses the headquarters of the Berkeley Unified School District. When the city began its landmark list in 1975, Old City Hall appeared at the top. The building forms part of the east-west axis of Civic Center Park. A fountain serves as the anchor and the Farm Credit Building across the way is the second part of the axis. The Veterans Memorial Building and the Berkeley Community Theater form the center's north-south axis.

This view of Center Street from Shattuck Avenue looks east toward the UC Berkeley campus with its signature Sather Tower, also called the Campanile. Architect John Galen Howard takes "center" stage here. Howard designed both the Sather Tower and the Berkeley National Bank Building (left foreground), where he maintained an office on the top floor. Howard was the university's supervising architect and the founder of the Department of Architecture. Peder and Jane Sather donated a considerable sum of money to the university. Both the Sather Gate (a memorial to Peder) and the Sather Tower (a memorial to Jane) reflect the couple's generosity. Howard based his design for the Campanile on one in Venice, Italy.

Today's view along Center Street juxtaposes the academic with the commercial. The Sather Tower on campus peeks around the Chamber of Commerce Building on Shattuck Avenue. In 1925, Walter Ratcliffe designed this as Berkeley's first skyscraper. Ratcliffe gave this Classic Revival building its signature three bands: light-colored stone at the base, dark red brick at the center, and a light terra cotta at the apex. The building housed the Berkeley Chamber of Commerce on its top floor until just before World War II. The eleven-story structure is popularly known as the Wells Fargo Building, for its ground-floor tenant since 1925.

A National Guard helicopter hovers over Sproul Plaza on the UC Berkeley campus on May 20, 1969, spraying tear gas indiscriminately on students and protestors alike. UC Berkeley had been a scene of counterculture ever since Mario Savio's Free Speech Movement was launched from Sproul Hall in 1964. In 1969 students were protesting over the university's plans to take back land it had earmarked for student housing between Haste Street, Dwight Way, and Bowditch Street, but had left undeveloped for years. The plan to ban tresspassers from "People's Park" backfired, and after angry clashes with the police, in which protestor James Rector was shot and killed, California Governor Ronald Reagan had to call out the National Guard (inset) to restore order.

Today Sproul Plaza is still a popular site for protests and political action, but not to the extremes of the militant 1960s. People's Park was eventually established as a public open space and Berkeley's Landmark Commission named the park a "Monument to Peace" in memory of James Rector and the people who were injured in the protest.

Sather Gate separates Sproul Plaza from the rest of the university. Jane K. Sather, a benefactor of the university, donated Sather Gate in memory of her late husband, the pioneering banker Peder Sather. Prominent Beaux Arts architect John Galen Howard designed the gate, which he completed in 1910. Professor Earl Cummins sculpted eight panels of bas-relief figures, with four nude men representing the disciplines of law, letters, medicine, and mining, and four naked women representing the disciplines of agriculture, architecture, art, and electricity. When Cummins first installed the panels, public outrage led Sather to demand their removal. Sather later funded the building of the Sather Tower, known more commonly as the Campanile because it bears a close resemblance to the Campanile de San Marco in Venice, Italy. It was also designed by Howard and was completed in 1914.

Originally the gate was at the terminus of Telegraph Avenue, marking the university's southern entrance. The circle in front of the gate acted as a turning point for the trolley cars coming from Oakland. However, the university later expanded further south and the gate became separated from Berkeley's city streets by the addition of Sproul Plaza. In 1977 the eight naked figures were rediscovered and reinstalled in their original positions. They can now be seen at the top of each pillar. Throughout the 1960s, UC Berkeley students gained a reputation for being politically outspoken, most notably their protests against the Vietnam War. Today Sather Gate still serves as a popular spot for handing out leaflets, public speaking, and politicking.

In 1900, cement contractor John Albert Marshall wanted to make a statement. He hired the firm of Cunningham Brothers to build this imposing Colonial Revival–style home, which he later sold. In 1904, Marshall had architect C. M. Cook design the Tudor Revival house next door. Marshall joined Cook and together they designed a series of homes in Berkeley: some as investments, others for Marshall to live in. One of their homes once stood on the site of People's Park. A stroll around Berkeley with a careful eye to the ground will reveal many of Marshall's construction stamps on the city's sidewalks. Architect Julia Morgan designed the third house on the block in 1907 for Joseph Mason of the real-estate firm Mason-McDuffie Co.

John Albert Marshall's two homes still stand. In 1979, the Colonial Revival home was purchased and converted into a bed-and-breakfast. Then, in 1984, the same owners purchased the Tudor Revival home and expanded their business. Both homes retain most of their interior and exterior architectural detailing. In 1991 they built a cottage house on the property. Joseph Mason's home no longer stands.

This 1892 photo of Shattuck Avenue seen from University Avenue shows the area just north of what was becoming downtown Berkeley. University Avenue served as a dividing line. The area south of this thoroughfare would develop from the nineteenth-century street, seen here, to a bustling downtown. The area north of University Avenue would develop more slowly. The Great San Francisco Earthquake and Fire in April 1906 changed everything. These wooden Victorian-era structures would soon vanish.

The area still retains its low-key Main Street atmosphere today with mostly one-story retail buildings lining Shattuck Avenue. The rail line that ran up Shattuck to Vine Street has been replaced to make room for buses and cars. Below the street, however, Bay Area Rapid Transit (BART) trains carry passengers. The downtown Berkeley BART stop is just a few blocks away from this intersection.

"Farms in Berkeley?" whimsically asked the ad for the Berkeley Farms Dairy. In this photo, taken when Berkeley Way was but a footpath, one can see that the answer must be yes. Even the cow that moos after the advertising jingle has a predecessor seen here, grazing contentedly in this bucolic setting. A close look on the horizon will reveal UC Berkeley's North Hall peeking over the trees to the right of the home and South Hall just to its right. North Hall no longer stands; it was razed in 1917 to make way for Wheeler Hall. South Hall still graces the campus as the only remaining building of the second phase of campus construction, which is known as architect David Farquharson's "picturesque phase."

This modern-day look up Berkeley Way from Martin Luther King Jr. Way shows the march of progress. A paved road has replaced the dirt path. A row of tall palm trees marks the location of Berkeley Bay Commons on Bonita Street. The building's architecture echoes its original use: William Black manufactured fireplaces. In 1905, he built the brick structure as a warehouse to store his bricks and plaster. Over the years, residents have used Bonita Hall as a regular meeting place. Berkeley Way today is a mixed-use street just off busy University Avenue.

Known as the "three-link fraternity" after the chain symbol visible on the pediment of the hall, the Odd Fellows were a fraternal organization that traced their roots back to England. This fellowship—whose three links stand for friendship, love, and truth—arrived in California with the gold rush and its members are still helping the citizens of California. A. H. Broad—who served Berkeley as town marshal—designed and built this structure for the Odd Fellows Berkeley Lodge No. 20 in 1884. Broad's company designed and built Eastlake cottages in both Oakland and Berkeley. This building, which was demolished in 1928, was one of the last Victorian-era structures on Shattuck Avenue.

In 1926 the Odd Fellows moved to their new temple on Fulton Street. The old Odd Fellows Hall remained vacant until it was demolished in July of 1928, likely the very last wooden structure on Shattuck Avenue. That same year, the Mason-McDuffie Real Estate Company built this Mediterranean Revival building in its place. The building stands today as a furniture showroom, a function well suited to the structure's two-story interior. The trees in the distance stand on UC Berkeley's campus.

Francisco and Gabriela Castro came to California from Mexico to settle on land that would one day comprise Richmond, San Pablo, El Sobrante, and El Cerrito. At one time, the Castro family owned this 19,000-acre ranch, Rancho San Pablo, where the Castro children grew up to marry and settle. Don Victor Castro built a two-story home in 1839 that would stand intact until 1956. He, his wife, and four children are buried in the same area. Juan Bautista Alvarado married Victor's sister, Martina, and ended up settling near San Pablo in 1848. Alvarado served as California's first native-born governor from 1836 to 1842.

After Don Victor's hacienda burned down in 1956, the city of El Cerrito eventually turned a large block of the city into a shopping center of massive proportions. The structure shown here represents a small part of today's El Cerrito Plaza Shopping Center. One adobe brick commemorates the site, which is also marked by a brass plaque. Castro's family also constructed an adobe in San Pablo center, which is today part of Richmond. The adobe was torn down in 1954 to make way for an apartment building. A replica of the adobe now serves as the San Pablo Museum of History.

Egbert Judson, an inventor and manufacturer of explosives, is said to have had the first assay house in San Francisco. He helped organize the San Francisco Chemical Works in 1867, when the company manufactured three pounds of dynamite with a trial test on boulders. This is considered the first manufacture and use of dynamite in the United States after Alfred Nobel invented it in 1866. The trial blast was successful enough to lead to the formation of the Giant Powder Co. Judson also formed the Judson Powder Co. and patented his "Giant Powder No. 2" in 1873. Not long after, Judson expanded to the edge of the water by what the Spanish called El Cerrito del Sur (Southern Little Hill). This explosion was captured in 1905.

Today, the addition of some plush condominiums to the side of the hill gives residents a pleasant view of the Golden Gate Fields and the bay. Golden Gate Fields, a popular Bay Area horse racetrack, has been on the site since February 1, 1941. While the city of El Cerrito took its name from this hill, the site lies within the borders of the city of Albany. As a result, some locals refer to the hill not as El Cerrito, but as Albany Hill.

The corner of Harbour Way and MacDonald Avenue represented the most prestigious location in downtown Richmond in 1930. The American Trust Building (later the Wells Fargo Bank) stands just up the street from the Hotel Carquinez, which is now on the National Register of Historic Places. Richmond's historic significance centers around the Kaiser-Permanente shipbuilding industry on the coast. Tremendous alterations to the tidal marshlands and Point Richmond Hills in the 1920s and 1930s gave rise to major industries, including a Ford Motor Company plant, Brickyard Cove, the Santa Fe Railroad, Kaiser-Permanente's four shipyards, and Winehaven, a major winery.

Part of Richmond's social significance centers around the role of women. The Women's West Side Improvement Club gave the city the basic services it needed early on. Later, in Henry Kaiser's shipyards, women would comprise one third of the workforce during World War II. Rosie the Riveter and her compatriots staffed many factories in Richmond and established new opportunities for women nationwide. The war boom hit Richmond harder than any other city in the East Bay, and once World War II was over, basic needs for housing and employment could not be met. The center of culture and business in Richmond since the turn of the nineteenth century, these two buildings still stand as testimony to the community's achievements.

Point Richmond's downtown, circa 1910, featured these three buildings that still stand today; each one is included on the National Register of Historic Places. The building at right, the Nicholl Building, served as Richmond's second city hall from 1909 to 1915. To the left of the Nicholl Building, Richmond's first bank and the Anderson Building formed the core of Richmond's first development. Originally called Eastyard, Point Richmond held the city's first fire department and hotel. The first hotel was also the location for the original city hall.

Today's Point Richmond looks much the same, with the Anderson Building still a significant part of downtown life. The building sold recently for $850,000. Incorporated in 1905, Richmond's goals have changed over the past hundred years. Once a booming industrial port city, Richmond now looks to its waterfront redevelopment as the key to attracting new residents, businesses, and visitors. By careful preservation of the historic district of Point Richmond and recent waterfront housing developments, Richmond may start bouncing back from its postwar decline.

The Women's West Side Improvement Club, formed in 1908 and still active today, took on the project of providing public drinking fountains. They built just one large fountain at the apex of the downtown triangle at Park Place and Washington Avenue. Ordered from the J. L. Mott Iron Works in San Francisco, the fountain structure featured an Indian statue on top. The statue, unveiled in 1909, presided over the business district until one night in 1943 when a local truck driver backed into the fountain, knocking the statue to the ground. The broken statue was probably used for the war effort. The fountain sat topless until 1984, when local contributors funded a new statue.

The Women's West Side Improvement Club also worked to bring Point Richmond a library, which eventually became a branch of the Richmond Library. The club would also make improvements to local parks. The replacement statue remains intact near the library, marking the center of historic Point Richmond. Much of the city's historic character remains here, completely isolated from the rest of Richmond's sprawling residential and industrial development to the east and north. It is still pedestrian-friendly, human-scaled, and uncongested.

In 1899 and 1900, construction crews bore into the hills west of Richmond to connect Richmond's factories to its active waterfront. By the spring of 1900, the Santa Fe Railroad had completely set up its operations in Richmond, including a ferry slip. Access to rail and water transportation and a burgeoning workforce made Richmond particularly desirable for factories; Standard Oil began its operations nearby in 1901. Standard Oil quickly grew to be the city's largest employer for many years to come. Job opportunities brought workers, and during the first decade of the twentieth century, the population grew from 2,000 to 10,000.

Augustin MacDonald, an early real-estate speculator, encouraged the Santa Fe Company to expand into Richmond. The main street downtown was named for MacDonald. The Santa Fe line continues to operate in town, running along Railroad Avenue just as it always has. Railroad Avenue gave rise to some of the seedier elements of Point Richmond, housing several brothels and saloons in the early part of the twentieth century. Regulations shut the local red-light district after World War II. The entire downtown area with its quaint shops is now on the National Register of Historic Places.

Chinese immigrants processed and exported dried shrimp to China from their shrimp camp near Point Richmond. They sold some of their catch locally and made a daily trek across the hills with huge buckets of fresh shrimp on either ends of poles slung over their shoulders. This image dates to 1904. The widespread immigration of new ethnic groups such as the Chinese and Italians led to a feeling of xenophobia in the last quarter of the nineteenth century, a feeling that reached its height in the 1920s. The Italians, Richmond's most highly represented ethnic group at the time, set up a wide range of small businesses in the city around the beginning of the twentieth century.

This shrimp camp was based at Point Molate Beach, which today is mostly deserted. It operated from 1865 to 1912, at which time the residents moved to more permanent living quarters. Following the 1906 earthquake, the California Wine Association moved its operation to Point Molate. The winery claimed to be the largest in the world until Prohibition forced the factory to close in 1920. Winehaven, built around 1907, still stands near the beach that once housed the shrimp camp; it is listed on the National Register of Historic Places.

The Richmond–San Rafael ferry began operations on May 1, 1905, with the ferry *Ellen*. The *Ellen* served only three months before being deemed unsafe and replaced with the much-larger *Charles Van Damme*. Prior to the opening, the only way to travel from Richmond to San Rafael required the use of two ferries: the first from Oakland to San Francisco, the second from San Francisco to Sausalito, a trip that required a good seven hours. The Richmond–San Rafael Ferry & Transportation Company continued operations until 1956, when the completion of the Richmond–San Rafael Bridge made its service obsolete.

Today, after much alteration of the natural shoreline and terrain, the spot where the ferry landing once operated is part of the Miller-Knox Regional Shoreline Ferry Point Park. Local residents fish and play next to the large structure that once served as the dock and waiting area for the ferry. During World War II, Richmond boomed. Industrialist Henry Kaiser built four major shipyards on the coast in addition to about 25,000 war housing units. By the middle of World War II, Richmond's population had quadrupled and housing overflowed. Ferry Point was a snarl of car traffic. By the late 1950s, though, the ferry slip and three of the four shipyards had closed.